Acts of Kindness

101 Ways to Make the World a Better Place

Rhonda Sciortino

hatherleigh
Improve your life. Change your world.

Improve your life. Change your world.

Hatherleigh Press is committed to preserving
and protecting the natural resources of the earth.
Environmentally responsible and sustainable practices
are embraced within the company's mission statement.

Visit us at www.hatherleighpress.com and register online
for free offers, discounts, special events, and more.

· ·
 ·

This book is dedicated to the best people in
the world—the authentically kind people.
You know who you are.

· ·
 ·

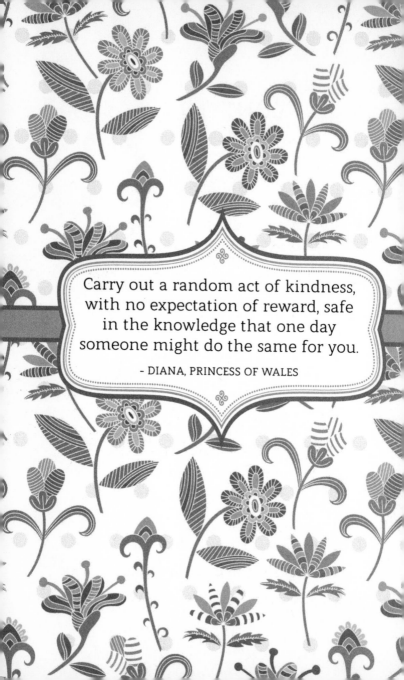

Carry out a random act of kindness,
with no expectation of reward, safe
in the knowledge that one day
someone might do the same for you.

- DIANA, PRINCESS OF WALES

CONTENTS

INTRODUCTION

From the simplest acts of kindness done for total strangers, to the most deliberate acts of kindness to those wounded souls who are the hardest to love—each act of kindness improves the lives of everyone involved.

When we hear about *random acts of kindness*, most of us will think, "*Oh, how nice.*" But we don't find ourselves moved to act in kind towards the people in our own lives. Whether it's because we're too busy, too focused, or too ill; whether it's because we think our kindness wouldn't make a difference or we just don't know *how* to show kindness, each of us can find a place in our lives for small, meaningful acts of kindness.

This book is all about showing you how to make your world a better place, regardless of your circumstances. Throughout these pages are woven all the wonderful reasons *why* we should engage in acts of kindness, so that by the time you've made your way through all 101 ways, YOU will be an *Ambassador of Kindness*, shining a spotlight on the best that humanity has to offer and setting an example for everyone about the awesome power of a simple act of kindness.

"Kindness is ever the begetter
of kindness."

–SOPHOCLES

KIND THINGS YOU CAN DO TODAY

"You cannot do a kindness too soon,
for you never know how soon it
will be too late."

–RALPH WALDO EMERSON

Notice something right where you are now.

Appreciate the beauty of it, and point it out to someone else. By doing this, you "put a pause" on whatever negativity is going on around you.

Forgive someone who hurt you.

It doesn't matter if they're still a part of your life, or if you can even find them to let them know you've forgiven them. Forgiveness isn't for them, it's for YOU.

Call a person you haven't spoken to in a while.

If you're not sure what to say, just say,
"Hi, I was thinking about you today.
How are you?"

Give a compliment.

Then *do* it! Focus on their character and ability, rather than on their physical appearance. You can say something like, *"I've noticed that you are a great listener,"* or, *"You seem like you genuinely care about your work. That's awesome!"*

Say a prayer for another person.

You don't have to be in a special place or in a specific posture. You can just say something simple like, "*God, please help my friend. You know what she needs. Thank you.*"

KIND THINGS YOU CAN DO FOR YOURSELF

"When you are kind to others,
it not only changes you,
it changes the world."

–HAROLD KUSHNER

6

Take a deep breath.

Hold it for a count of five seconds,
and slowly exhale. Be grateful that
you can do that.

7

Smile.

When you smile, chemicals are released in your brain that literally make you feel better. Not to mention, smiling is contagious. Your smile can start a domino effect of grins that gets passed on to brighten the days of many.

8

Remind yourself of your strongest character trait.

It could be your integrity, resilience, resourcefulness, courage, etc. Say to yourself ten times, *"I am courageous!"* Or, *"I am resilient!"* Then add, *"I like myself!"* You won't be able to do this without smiling!

Help someone who really needs it.

Sometimes, one of the most rewarding things you can do for yourself is to help someone who really needs it—especially someone who would never ask for help, and who expects nothing from you.

10

Forgive yourself.

Forgive yourself for anything you've said, done, or even thought, that you aren't proud of. Then let it go. Don't think of it or speak of it again.

KIND THINGS YOU CAN DO FOR OTHERS

"Never look down on anybody
unless you're helping him up."

–JESSE JACKSON

11

Teach another person how to do something that comes naturally to you.

While it may seem like you're teaching them something simple or obvious, sharing your unique talents with others can open up whole new avenues of opportunity for them.

Ask someone their opinion on something.

By asking someone what they think about something, you show them that you value their input.

Make eye contact with everyone you speak with.

Resist the temptation to look around, glance at your watch, or "multi-task" while you are with others. Making eye contact says, *"You are worthy of my attention."*

14

Listen.

One of the most powerful things you can do to enhance relationships and improve your life is to listen to others and really hear what they say. When you get good at this, you will begin to better understand where they're coming from, and even what they leave unsaid.

15

Do not interrupt.

Interrupting others, even to ask questions about what they're telling you, is rude. (If you are pressed for time, say, *"I'm so sorry; I care about you, but I have to go."*) Resisting the temptation to interrupt will give you more information, deeper insight into the person, and may just answer your questions or address any comments you wanted to share.

Kind things you can do for family

"Every day of our lives we are given opportunities to show love and kindness to those around us."

–THOMAS MONSON

16

Ask them about their best childhood memories.

Listen to and observe what they say and show you. Watch facial expressions and body language, and you may garner meaningful insight into the person, thereby enhancing your relationships.

Engage with older family members.

Ask older family members what, in their opinion, has changed most in the world during their lifetimes. The perspectives of those who have been a part of this world longer than you have are invaluable.

Ask what they would do, if they could do anything.

Don't assume you know; there may be a secret dream or desire hidden in their hearts that they've never spoken aloud.

Organize a family picnic, celebration, or reunion.

Make a special effort to reach out to distant relatives you don't regularly connect with, and those who are seldom included. If they choose not to attend, that's okay, but be sure they know they've been invited.

Create a shared tradition.

Doing so encourages a sense of
camaraderie and builds a concrete
example of the bond between you and
those you care about, that everyone can
participate in and enjoy.

KIND THINGS YOU CAN DO FOR YOUR NEIGHBORHOOD

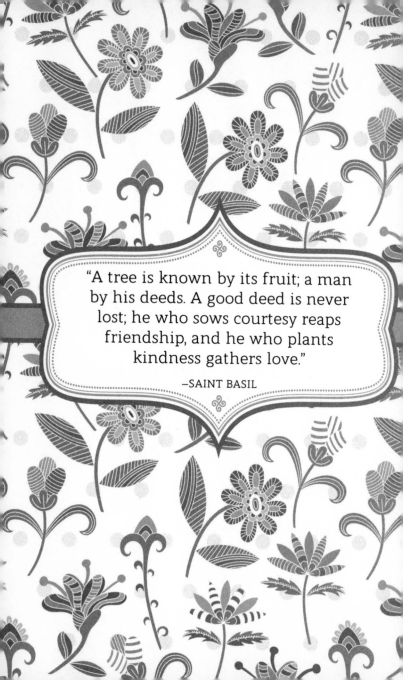

"A tree is known by its fruit; a man by his deeds. A good deed is never lost; he who sows courtesy reaps friendship, and he who plants kindness gathers love."

–SAINT BASIL

Volunteer.

Volunteer with a community service
or faith-based organization in your
community. Offer to do something that
comes easily to you or that you've been
trained to do, or else try something that
is brand new to you.

Be a neighbor who looks out for others.

This especially applies to those who are too young, elderly, or medically vulnerable to take care of themselves.

Organize a neighborhood potluck.

Personally invite neighbors who don't normally engage with the rest of the neighborhood.

Host a chili cook-off.

Engage the whole community in cooking
and tasting.

25

"Catch" people doing good!

When you observe someone performing their own random act of kindness, call it out. By calling attention to and praising the good deeds done by others, you make kindness more visible, and thus more common.

KIND THINGS YOU CAN DO AT WORK

"No act of kindness, no matter how small, is ever wasted."

—AESOP

26

Take the initiative.

Ask if there is something extra that you
can do to add more value to the product
or service offered by your employer.

27

Do something special for your co-workers.

A great example is to bake cookies for your co-workers (making sure to check for any allergies!)

28

Start everyone's day with a smile.

Work to earn a reputation as the person who greets everyone cheerfully each morning.

Notice when others are having a bad day.

Take the time to offer a word of encouragement or tell a joke that lightens the mood.

Give 100%.

Set aside your concerns, and focus
solely on using your unique set of skills,
talents, and abilities to further the
mission of the organization.

Kind things you can do for total strangers

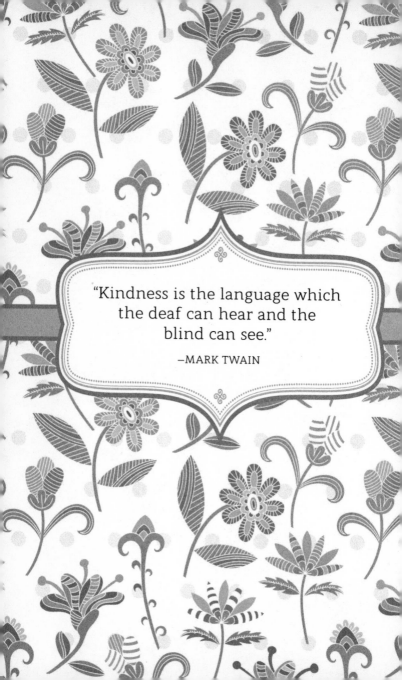

"Kindness is the language which the deaf can hear and the blind can see."

—MARK TWAIN

31

Smile and wave at passers-by.

They'll either smile and wave back, or think you're nuts, but either way it gets you smiling!

32

Say, "Hello!"

This may sound completely insignificant,
but you'll be surprised how many
people walk right past others as though
they're not living, breathing people with
thoughts and feelings of their own.
Ignoring others diminishes their worth;
even if the other person is ignoring you,
be the one who says hello.

Hold the door for someone.

When you're walking in or out of a building, check around you to see if anyone else is coming toward that door, and hold the door open. Never be the person who allows a door to slam in someone's face.

When you see someone struggling, offer to help.

Even the offer of a helping hand can be enough to improve someone's day. If we all learn to help the person next to us, the world will be a better place overnight!

Let someone go ahead of you in line.

Make space for another person in line, or on the bus, or in the subway, especially if they appear more fragile than you are.

KIND THINGS YOU
CAN DO FOR
FRIENDS

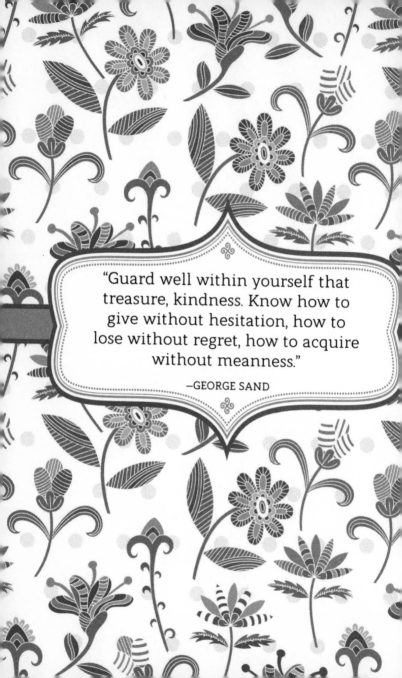

"Guard well within yourself that treasure, kindness. Know how to give without hesitation, how to lose without regret, how to acquire without meanness."

—GEORGE SAND

36

Remember birthdays.

Call, send a card, text, or send your regards through social networking, but don't miss the opportunity to tell your friends that you celebrate the anniversary of the day they arrived on Earth.

37

Learn about their beliefs.

Everyone has beliefs and values they
hold dear. Your friends may have some
of the same beliefs and values that you
do, or they may be wildly different.
Either way, ask and sincerely listen
without arguing or trying to persuade
them of your point of view.

38

Stay in touch.

Don't let too much time go by without texting, calling, or getting together with the ones you care about. Be the one who makes the effort to nurture good relationships.

39

Remind them what you like about them.

Do you admire their ability to gracefully entertain? Are you inspired by their tenacity in the face of adversity? Have you noticed the way they resolve conflict with others?

40

Tell them how they have contributed to your life.

Remind them of times when they cheered you up and were there for you when you needed a friend. Tell them the lessons they taught you with their words or actions. They may be completely unaware that they've contributed to your life, and hearing it from you will enrich them.

KIND THINGS YOU CAN DO AT HOME

"Anyone can find the dirt in someone. Be someone who finds the gold."

—PROVERBS 11:27

41

Keep yourself organized.

It's easier to be kind when you
aren't stressed about clutter and
disorganization. So, organize your life!
Having a file folder or notebook for
your important papers, bills, receipts,
and records can save you time and
frustration and let you use that energy
to be kind instead.

Donate to others what you don't need for yourself.

Giving away what you no longer use shows kindness to others and simplifies your life. Ask yourself: do you really need *three* potato peelers? Or those sweaters in the back of your closet? Donate them, or toss out anything that makes it difficult to find what you really need. That way, you'll have the "bandwidth" necessary to turn your attention towards practicing a life of intentional kindness.

Offer to do someone's laundry.

Offering to do someone's laundry, or hem a pair of pants, or even just sew on a button, is a little act of kindness that shows someone you're thinking of them.

Make your favorite dish and invite someone to dinner.

Inviting someone into your home is tantamount to letting them into your "safe place," and thereby your heart. And when you open the door to your heart, you enrich your life.

Do something you enjoy that can be shared with others.

For example, do you have the best recipe for chocolate chip cookies? Bake your awesome cookies, and then wrap some cookies in cello-wrap, tie a bow around the top, and give them to everyone you see during the next 24 hours.

KIND THINGS YOU CAN DO THAT COST NOTHING

"Spread love everywhere you go.
Let no one ever come to you
without leaving happier."

—MOTHER TERESA

Invite a friend to go for a walk with you.

Sharing your time with someone, keeping them company and enjoying the outside world together, can completely transform a person's day.

Tell someone, "I'm so glad you're in my life."

We're all precious to someone, but it never hurts to hear it! These simple words can improve a person's day, deepen a friendship, or confirm a relationship.

48

Give a hug, a handshake, or just a quick wink.

Physical contact allows you to really connect with a person, letting them know you appreciate them without a single word spoken.

Make a list of people you care about.

One by one, tell each of them how much you care about them. Having this list on hand can make you really appreciate how blessed you are.

Read a book to a person who can't do it themselves.

This can be a child, someone in the hospital, or someone in a convalescent facility.

KIND THINGS YOU CAN DO WITH WORDS

"Kindness in words creates confidence. Kindness in thinking creates profoundness. Kindness in giving creates love."

—LAO TZU

51

Ask about a person's deepest dream.

Everyone has one. When we ask others about their dreams, aspirations, or goals, we show them that we care about what *they* care about, and we are giving them permission and a space to pull that dream out and discuss it, in vivid color.

Give advice.

When you want to correct someone, find a private place to have the conversation, and begin with, *"I care about you, and I want you to be happy, so...."* Always correct someone or give advice privately.

53

Praise others.

Identify a good character trait, recognize
good behavior, or celebrate a great
attitude by praising others. When
possible, do this in the presence of
others. What gets praised is more likely
to be repeated. So recognize and reward
the good character traits, attitudes, and
behaviors you want to see repeated.

54

Share your story.

Share your dreams, your mistakes, and your triumphs with the people around you. When we open our hearts and share the things we care most about, we open ourselves to others, inviting them into our hearts and giving them permission to share their stories with us.

Ask someone, "What would have to happen for you to be happy today?"

When we pose this question, the human brain automatically begins to calculate answers. Just asking this one question can stimulate people to think realistically about what they can do to feel happiness then and there—not in some vague, distant time in the future, but right NOW. Sometimes, people discover that happiness is as simple as making the decision to be happy.

KIND THINGS YOU CAN DO WITHOUT WORDS

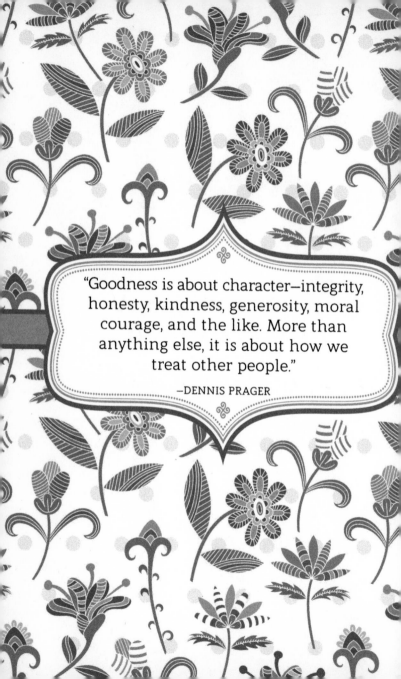

"Goodness is about character—integrity, honesty, kindness, generosity, moral courage, and the like. More than anything else, it is about how we treat other people."

—DENNIS PRAGER

56

Smile with your whole face.

Smile like you would with a baby
when hoping that the baby will
mimic your smile. No one can resist
smiling when faced with an authentic,
enthusiastic smile.

Reach out and gently touch the back of someone's hand.

Touching someone in this way shows symbolically that you are joining that person in his or her emotional space.

58

Hold hands.

Holding hands or linking pinkie fingers shows that you are "doing life" together in that moment.

Send someone a picture that shows how much you like them.

Let them know through a picture how delighted you are about their success and how much you look forward to seeing them. Remember, a picture is worth a thousand words!

When talking, lean forward slightly.

This shows through your body language that you are actively listening to what he or she has to say.

KIND THINGS
YOU CAN DO
SPONTANEOUSLY

"Be kind whenever possible.
It is always possible."

–DALAI LAMA

61

Smile and wave at people around you, whether you know them or not!

By doing that, you become the one who warms up the world.

Provide lunch to a person who would otherwise go without.

If there is a place where you regularly see homeless people, carry a jar of peanut butter, a loaf of bread, and a plastic fork in a bag in it in your car, ready to give away.

63

Carry "kindness cards" to give out to people.

You can purchase little cards, the size of a business card or smaller, that have pre-printed hopeful, encouraging, or inspirational sentiments on them. The point of putting kindness into writing is that people can keep it and be encouraged by it long after their encounter with you.

After you've read an enjoyable book or magazine, give it away.

You can leave magazines and books at a retirement home or community center or donate them to a public library (or even some post offices) for the enjoyment of others.

65

Clean out your closet.

Take gently used items to a local homeless shelter or a community clothing closet.

KIND THINGS YOU CAN DO AROUND THE HOLIDAYS

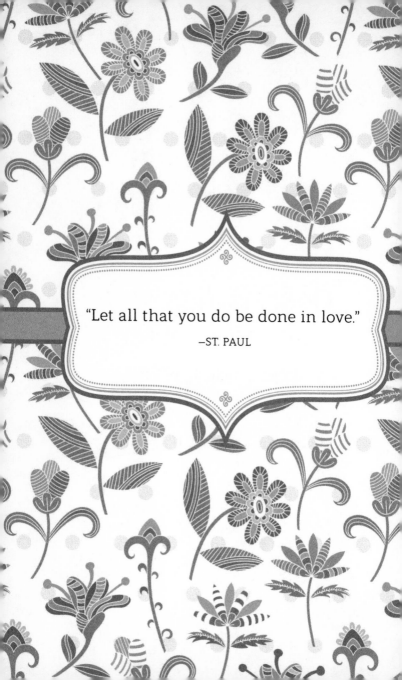

"Let all that you do be done in love."

—ST. PAUL

66

Go caroling.

Go caroling through a neighborhood or at a children's hospital or retirement home. Invite friends, family, and neighbors to join in. The more, the merrier!

67

Throw a costume party or theme party.

Have the group vote for the best costume or "truest to theme" winner.

Make the holidays easier for others.

Holidays are difficult for some people. If you are one of those people, organize an "anti-holiday" or a made-up-holiday get-together. Borrowing from an old *Seinfeld* episode, you can organize a *"Festivus for the Rest of Us!"*

Send a homemade photo card.

Photo cards are convenient, but can appear impersonal. Customize your cards by handwriting and signing a note, photographing your note, and uploading the photograph onto the card for a personal touch of kindness.

70

Give someone a call around the holidays.

Holiday cards are a great way to stay in touch, but phone calls are even better! Call people you haven't spoken to in a while to wish them a happy holiday, and to let them know you're thinking of them.

KIND THINGS YOU CAN DO FOR ACQUAINTANCES

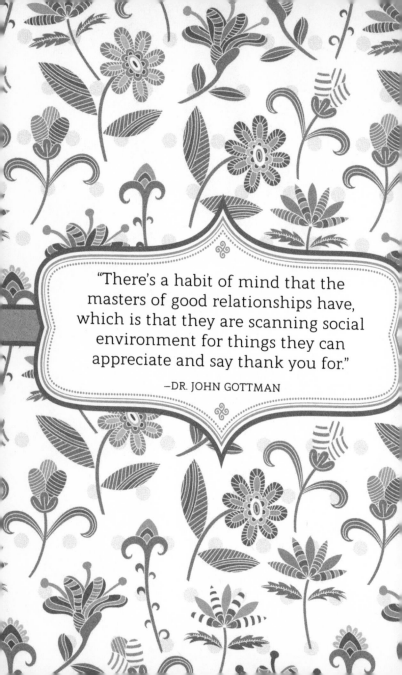

"There's a habit of mind that the masters of good relationships have, which is that they are scanning social environment for things they can appreciate and say thank you for."

—DR. JOHN GOTTMAN

Give someone the benefit of the doubt.

When you hear something negative about someone you don't know well, give that person the benefit of the doubt rather than automatically accepting the negative conclusions of others.

72

Go to coffee with an acquaintance.

A friendship may blossom, or it may not; either way, when asked the right questions, everyone is interesting for an hour. Here's a hint: one of the "right questions" is, *"Please tell me about yourself."*

Be determined to learn from everyone you meet.

Everyone has something to teach, whether they are aware of it or not. It could be a lesson on how *not* to behave, but there is still a lesson to be learned from everyone.

Spend more time listening than talking.

If you actively listen, you may find areas of common interest, shared values or beliefs, or similar hopes and dreams. It is on these things that relationships can be built, and good relationships enrich the soul.

75

Determine to leave people better than you found them.

You can do this with your acquaintances by giving them hope. Hope is built through encouragement and inspiration, so be ready with words meant to encourage and inspire.

KIND THINGS YOU CAN DO FOR CHILDREN

"Tenderness and kindness are not signs of weakness and despair, but manifestations of strength and resolution."

— KHALIL GIBRAN

76

Teach a child to do something you know how to do.

First show him or her, and then watch him or her do the task. Afterwards, show—don't just tell—them any necessary corrections.

77

Invite a child to join you in doing something you enjoy.

Children are naturally curious about the adult world, and sharing something you love with them can instill in them an appreciation for all the opportunities the world offers.

Help to teach the child about the world.

Children have their own misapprehensions about how the world works, and from time to time need to be corrected. Remember that each time you move to correct a child, begin every correction with, *"I care about you and want you to be happy."*

79

Ask children what they think about current events.

Really listen to their responses, ask follow-up questions, and then offer your thoughts. This lets you in on their thought processes, alerts you to any errant conclusions they may have, and gives you an opportunity to share with them your thoughts as a positive influence.

Explain decisions to children in an age-appropriate way.

This teaches them critical thinking and discerning skills so they'll be able to make good decisions even when you're not around.

KIND THINGS YOU CAN DO FOR TEENS

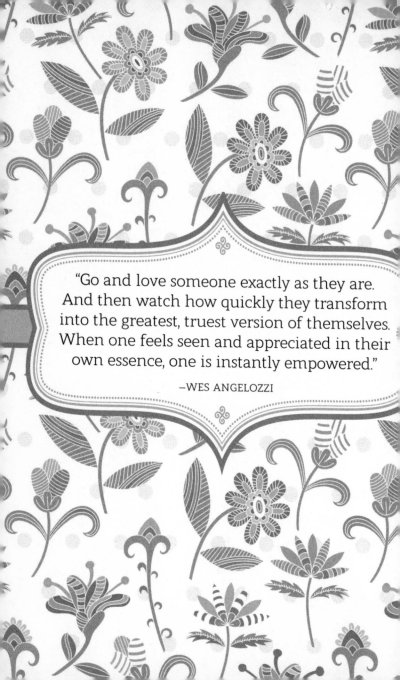

"Go and love someone exactly as they are. And then watch how quickly they transform into the greatest, truest version of themselves. When one feels seen and appreciated in their own essence, one is instantly empowered."

—WES ANGELOZZI

81

Set aside time for the teens in your life.

In the chaos of imbalanced hormones, peer pressure, and rapidly changing culture, you can create much-needed stability in the life of a teen by having a regularly scheduled "date." Whether it's once a week or once a month, make standing dates with the teens in your life, and then follow through, regardless of their behaviors or attitudes.

82

Share your values, while respecting their own.

Rather than preach to teens, try to give them engaging books or share compelling videos that represent the values you hope to share with them.

Take teens to work with you.

Be sure to explain the mission and vision of the company so they understand not just *what* you do, but *why* you do that work.

84

Schedule informational trips to local businesses.

Get permission from business owners to take teens on "how it's done" outings at manufacturing plants, auto repair shops, and other hands-on type businesses to give them an understanding of what it takes to produce a product or service. This teaches them how things get done and gives them a glimpse of (and respect for) the work involved in those jobs.

85

Give teens jobs to do, and offer them pay.

This lets teens earn their own money,
and teaches them to save, invest, and
to spend wisely. If they learn to do
that with small amounts of money,
doing it with larger amounts later
will come easily.

KIND THINGS YOU CAN DO FOR YOUNG ADULTS

"Be somebody who makes
everybody feel like somebody."

—ANONYMOUS

Offer to be a mentor.

Work to help them through the inevitable bumps on their road to authentically successful lives.

Be willing to share the life lessons you have learned.

By doing so, you ensure that they are better able to avoid the pitfalls in life that are preventable and foreseeable.

Be willing to listen first.

Share only when you sense they're
ready to receive. Remember that young
adults don't have the wisdom that
you've acquired along the way. Giving
unsolicited wisdom before a young adult
is ready to hear it could be a waste of
your time and energy.

Write a letter, or take a video of yourself.

A written document or a recorded video will be available for them to take in time and again. And, perhaps most importantly, it will always be there when they most need to hear what you have to say.

90

Start an "advice project."

Ask friends and colleagues to write or video their best bit of advice to a young adult. Compile the advice you receive into a scrapbook or CD, and give it to the young adult. This will be a priceless asset, one that is both a keepsake and a useful tool.

Kind things you can do for people going through tough times

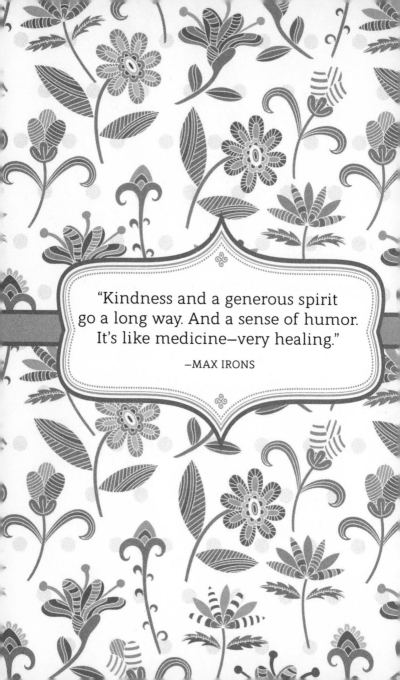

"Kindness and a generous spirit go a long way. And a sense of humor. It's like medicine—very healing."

—MAX IRONS

91

Acknowledge the pain of others.

Although understanding someone's pain doesn't fix the problem, it does help to know that there is someone who cares about what you're going through.

92

Remind them this present adversity will pass.

It may pass like a large kidney stone, but it will pass!

Overlook irritability.

When people are under pressure or are in pain, their ability to be kind to others diminishes or disappears entirely. One of the greatest kindnesses you can show to a person who is in the midst of adversity is to ignore bad attitudes, rude comments, and hurtful actions.

94

Help them recognize options they may not have considered.

Reinforce the truth that everyone always has choices—especially when we think we don't. It's easy to get stuck in a difficult situation, thinking that there is no way out or only one way out. Since you're on the outside looking in, it's easier for you to identify possible ways out of their painful circumstances.

95

Give them a break from their circumstances.

Take him or her to a movie, out to lunch, a comedy show, or to some totally unrelated kind of gathering—anything to temporarily move their focus off of their problems and onto something else.

KIND THINGS YOU CAN DO TO IMPROVE THE WORLD

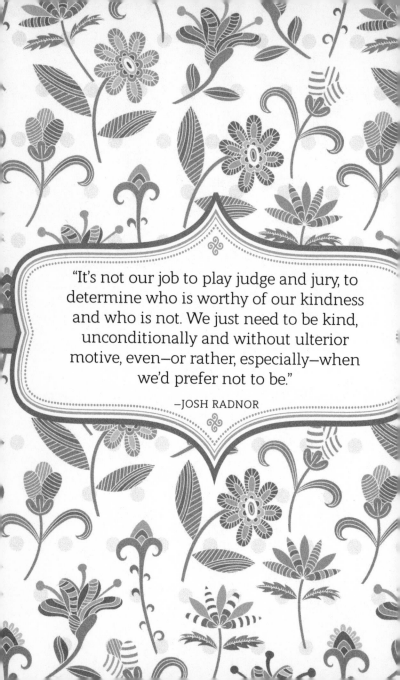

"It's not our job to play judge and jury, to determine who is worthy of our kindness and who is not. We just need to be kind, unconditionally and without ulterior motive, even—or rather, especially—when we'd prefer not to be."

—JOSH RADNOR

96

Act like a likable person, until you no longer have to act!

Remember: a likable person is a kind person.

Be generous!

Decide to give something of yourself
every day, whether it's a smile, a kind
word, a word of encouragement,
half of your lunch, anonymously
paying for someone's meal, or giving
away something you still enjoy. Your
generosity will make both the giver and
the recipient feel good.

98

Be mindful of your words and actions.

Your attitude, words, and behaviors change *you* as well as the atmosphere around you. When you change yourself and the atmosphere around you, you model that behavior for others, and inspire them to do the same.

99

Learn to sympathize with those who wrong you.

When someone says or does something that leaves you feeling offended, rather than taking offense, feel sympathy for the perceived offender. His or her words are a clear indicator of that person's character or emotional state.

Choose to be optimistic.

By doing that, you'll be doing everyone
the kindness of modeling how to be
positive. The best part is that by doing so,
you make it more likely that everything
will work out beautifully.

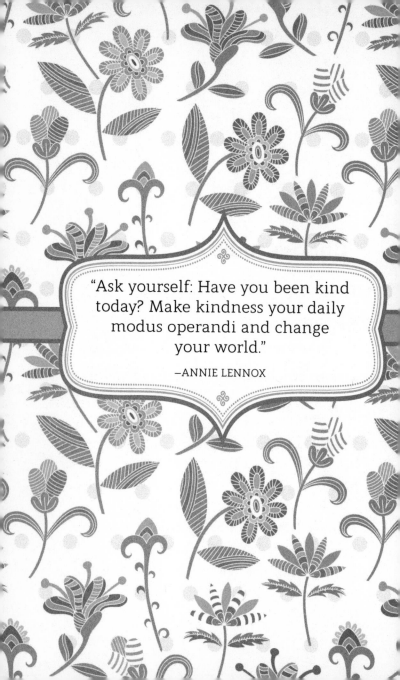

"Ask yourself: Have you been kind today? Make kindness your daily modus operandi and change your world."

–ANNIE LENNOX

Put these words into action.

By now, you know that there are an unlimited number of ways to show kindness. For every "pain point" in life, there are acts of kindness that can make things better, ranging from the smallest, nearly insignificant gestures to the deepest, most profound good works.

The miraculous aspect of kindness is that when you decide to live a life of kindness, the energy from which you give kindness is not depleted; rather, it grows. When you deliberately give kindness, whether it's a simple wink to a mom struggling with a toddler in the grocery store or the "all-in" act of taking in a friend who has nowhere else to go, *giving kindness enriches your life.*

After all, a simple act of kindness from you might be the answer to someone's greatest need. For example, someone who happens to be a "natural" at doing hair and makeup could get the daughter of a single mom dolled up for the prom in a way that mom could never afford. A mechanic could make a simple repair that provides an unemployed person the transportation necessary to get a job. For every task that you can easily and quickly do, there is someone in your community who needs or desires that to be done. When you connect your acts of kindness with someone that has that specific need, the result is a kindness explosion! You feel a sense of fulfillment that your talents were valuable to someone else, and the recipient of your kindness is now better enabled to pass on his or her own acts of kindness in an endless chain of good will and good works.

Whether you are someone who has practiced kindness throughout your entire life or someone who hasn't ever given it any serious thought, consider setting off an explosion of kindness in your life, your family, your neighborhood, your workplace, and everywhere else you go. You can do this by challenging yourself and others to find new ways to practice kindness, to recognize and celebrate kindness, and to model for others how to practice basic good will. You can even organize a "Kindness Club" in your neighborhood, workplace, family, church, school, or other social group. Share ideas, organize events, invite people who aren't typically included, engage with leaders, and connect with social services organizations to learn who in your community most needs kindness and how you can enhance kindness efforts that are already happening .

And so, my challenge to you is to go make the world a better place!

RESOURCES

For guidance on bringing a Kindness Explosion to your community, go to www.faithismotion.org.

For guidance on being kind to people who are unable to reciprocate, read *How to Hug a Porcupine*.

For a program to help people help themselves, go to www.yourrealsuccess.com.

About the Author

Rhonda Sciortino is an author, motivational speaker and coach for authentic success. She overcame abuse, homelessness, and poverty to become a successful entrepreneur, spokeswoman, and advocate for abused children. She currently serves as the chair for the Successful Survivors Foundation, an organization created to help survivors of adversity to create personal and professional success. Rhonda lives in Southern California with her husband, Nick, near their daughter and her family. Additional information is available at www.rhonda.org.

Also by Rhonda Sciortino

How to Get to Awesome

Successful Survivors

Also from Chatherleigh

. . . .
. . . .

The Book Lover's Treasury of Quotations

The Cat Lover's Quotation Book

Celebrate Love

The Dog Lover's Quotation Book

A Garden of Inspiration

How to Hug a Porcupine

Mindfulness in Nature

The Need to Say No

When I Look to the Sky

Available where books are sold